THE DANUBE

Written and photographed by

David Cumming

Wayland

THE WORLD'S RIVERS

The Amazon
The Danube
The Ganges
The Mississippi
The Nile
The Rhine
The Seine
The Thames
The Volga
The Yellow River

Cover *A view of the River Danube as it flows through the city of Budapest.*

Series and book editor Rosemary Ashley
Series designer Derek Lee
Book designer John Yates

First published in 1993 by
Wayland (Publishers) Limited
61 Western Road, Hove
East Sussex, BN3 1JD, England

**British Library Cataloguing in
Publication Data**
Cumming, David
    Danube.—(World's Rivers Series)
    I. Title II. Series
    914.96

ISBN 0-7502-0773-6

Typeset in the UK by
Dorchester Typesetting Group Ltd
Printed in Italy by G. Canale C.S.p.A.

CONTENTS

1. 'THE MIGHTIEST OF RIVERS'

The Austrian composer, Johann Strauss, made the River Danube famous. In 1867, unsure of what to call a waltz he had just written, he named it after the river near his home in Vienna. Today *The Blue Danube Waltz* is hummed all over the world. If it were not for this tune, many of us would probably never have heard of the River Danube.

For much of its route, the Danube is the border between two countries, either flowing through or past all of the following: Germany, Austria, Slovakia (part of what used to be called Czechoslovakia), Hungary, Croatia and Serbia (in what was formerly Yugoslavia), Romania, Bulgaria and Ukraine. No other river in the world is connected with so many countries.

Although not the longest river in Europe, the Danube is certainly the most powerful and fastest flowing, for no other European river carries so much water. Over three hundred tributaries add their waters to the Danube, including all the rivers of Romania, 75 per cent of those in the old Yugoslavia (before it split into separate countries) and most of those in Austria. Once, terrible floods were common as the Danube's banks could not hold all the water pouring down between them. The force of this water was so

Budapest, in Hungary, is one of the three capital cities through which the Danube flows.

4

powerful that huge whirlpools were formed when it hit underwater rocks, and many a boat and crew vanished in their depths. No wonder then that Herodotus, a Greek historian in the fifth century BC, described the Danube as 'the mightiest of rivers'. At that time it was thought to be the largest and most destructive river in the world — and only the very bravest attempted to journey down it.

Today, the river is no longer fierce. With the help of a chain of huge dams, the Danube has been tamed. Floods are rare and even the smallest boats can travel along it safely. In the future, perhaps, the Danube will develop like its neighbour, the River Rhine, and become one of the busiest waterways in the world — especially as the two rivers are now joined together.

In September 1992, a canal linking the Rivers Rhine, Main and Danube was opened in southern Germany, making it possible for a barge to travel from the North Sea to the Black Sea. Since carrying goods by water is much cheaper than by road or rail, many businesses in Europe, in the Commonwealth of Independent States or CIS (formerly the USSR) and in the countries around the Black Sea, may switch to this means of transport. If they do, then the Danube will become a busy waterway. However, it will take many years for this trade to develop. Until then, traffic on the Danube will build up slowly.

Facts and figures about the Danube
Source: A spring at Donaueschingen in the Black Forest region of southern Germany, 678 m above sea level.
Length: 2,880 km; the 25th longest river in the world and the second longest in Europe, after the Volga in Russia.
Drainage basin: 816,000 sq km (more than 3 times the size of the UK).
Delta area: 4,152 sq km, most of which is on Romania's Black Sea coast and a small part in Ukraine.
Water outflow at mouth: 5,886 cubic metres per second, which is the highest in Europe — over twice the amount flowing out of the Volga and almost four times the amount flowing out of the Rhine.
Tributaries: over 300.
Different names: Donau (German), Dunaj (Slovak), Duna (Hungarian), Duna (Serbo-Croat), Dunarea (Romanian), Dunay (Russian), Danubius (Latin), Hister (ancient Greek).

A cross-section of the Danube's course, showing how far it drops on its journey to the Black Sea.

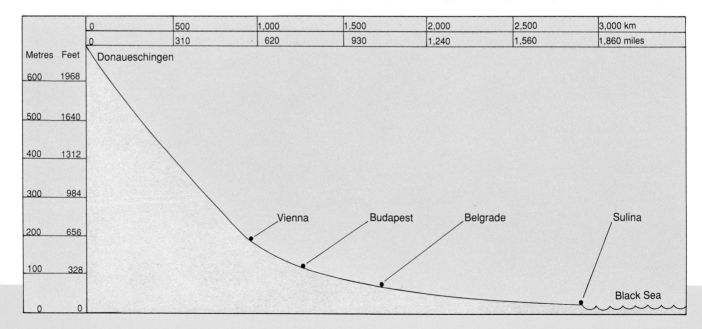

2. FROM THE BLACK FOREST TO THE BLACK SEA

The upper Danube

The Danube begins its long journey to the Black Sea in the hilly region of south-western Germany called the Black Forest. Here, two streams, the Brigach and Breg, descend from the highlands to meet at Donaueschingen and become the Danube. Nearby, in the grounds of an old palace belonging to the Fürstenberg family, there is a spring which trickles into the Brigach. The Fürstenbergs claim that this is the true source of the Danube because it never dries up, whereas the Breg and Brigach streams do dry up in summers when there is little rain. Even so, geographers still consider the confluence of the Breg and Brigach to be the starting-point. And since the Breg rises furthest away from the Danube's delta, this is where the river really begins.

Left *The spring in the grounds of the Fürstenberg Palace, in Donaueschingen, which many people say is the real source of the river because it never dries up.*

Right *Geographers argue that the confluence of the Breg and Brigach rivers, shown here, is where the Danube begins.*

Sigmaringen Castle overlooks the river from its position on the top of a rocky outcrop.

From Donaueschingen, the Danube heads north-eastwards to the Swabian Hills. Just before it reaches them, it disappears. Near Immendingen, cracks in the river bed have been made bigger by the action of the river flowing over them. Much of the Danube vanishes through the cracks into channels deep underground in the limestone rock, to reappear a few kilometres away in Switzerland, in a tributary of the River Rhine. Sometimes there is so little rain in summer that all the water goes down the cracks and people can walk along the river bed. In most years, though, there is enough water for the river to continue on its way.

The Danube twists and turns through the Swabian Hills. This is one of the most exciting parts of the river's route, with beautiful, narrow wooded valleys leading into deep gorges, their steep sides dotted with large outcrops of rocks, weathered over the centuries into odd, often frightening, shapes. Guarding the entrance to most of these valleys and gorges is a castle, perched on the edge so that its soldiers could have a clear view all around them. Some of the castles are in ruins; others have been restored and converted into hotels or museums.

East of the Swabian Hills, the land flattens and the Danube's valley, no longer squeezed between high-sided limestone cliffs, widens as it approaches Ulm, the first city along its course. By now the Danube looks like a major river. It is 20 m wide and 1 m deep, and small barges can use it for transporting goods. Larger barges start to use the river further along, at Kelheim, for by this stage the Rivers Iller and Lech have joined the Danube and raised the level of water. At Kelheim the River Altmuhl also enters the Danube. The point where the Altmuhl enters the river is the southern end of the canal that now links the Rhine and the Danube.

Just downstream from Kelheim is the first of the many dams and locks which have been built to control the water flowing down the Danube. These keep the river deep enough for barges to use all year round, so from this point on the Danube is an international waterway, along which barges can travel up and downriver to the Black Sea. Once, they started and finished their journeys at Regensburg, downriver from Kelheim, as its harbour was as far inland as they could go.

Today, thanks to the new canal, barges can continue up to Frankfurt and the ports on the River Rhine. Regensburg is the most northern point on the Danube, and once past it the river bends south to the border between Germany and Austria at Passau.

The spire of Ulm Cathedral is 161m high. It is the tallest cathedral spire in the world.

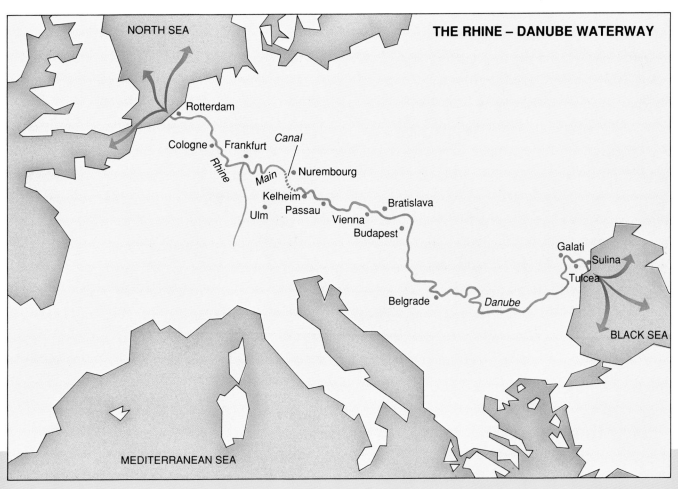

9

Not only do two countries meet at Passau, but also three rivers. One of the Danube's largest tributaries, the Inn from Austria, joins it here along with one of its smallest tributaries, the Ilz from the Czech republic. In fact, the Inn carries more water than the Danube at Passau, especially in spring when it is swollen with the icy water from the melting snows of the Alps. This water rushes down from the mountains with such force that it pushes into the Danube for several hundred metres before the two rivers merge into one. In spring

Left *The blue, icy waters of the Inn flow alongside the darker Danube, before the two rivers join together.*

Below *Attractive, modernized old houses overlook the weir at Riedlingen in Austria. Many dams and weirs were built along the Danube to control the powerful flow of the river.*

One of the most beautiful stretches of the Danube; the gently sloping hills of the Wachau Valley in Austria, just north of Vienna.

1954, the weather was unusually hot and the snow melted very quickly, raising the water in the Inn to such a high level that it burst its banks and cut across to the nearby Danube, turning Passau into an island with all the lower floors of its buildings under water.

After crossing into Austria, the river's valley shrinks again, twisting and turning as it is squeezed between ranges of tree-covered hills, many of them crowned by the ruins of ancient castles, reminders of bygone times when bishops, princes and noblemen fought each other for control of this area. At Linz, the valley opens up once more and the Danube winds among the gentle slopes of the hills in the Wachau Valley, one of the prettiest sections of the river, before arriving at Vienna, the capital of Austria.

North of Budapest, the river flows east before turning sharply south across the flat lands of the Great Hungarian Plain.

The middle Danube

So far, the Danube has been a highland river, flowing through a series of narrow, high-sided valleys. Its current, too, has been strong, as it has been descending steeply: between Passau and Vienna, for example, it drops 1 m every 2 km.

However, below Vienna, the character of the river starts to change. From here to its delta the Danube travels across gently sloping land: between Vienna and the Black Sea it falls less than 1 m every 10 km. With such a gentle rate of descent, the current slows and the Danube starts to drop the silt brought down from the mountains by its tributaries. Below Bratislava, on the border between Austria and Slovakia, the silt has built up to form islands, sometimes up to 90 km long and 45 km wide, which block the flow of water, forcing the river to split into several channels.

Soon after Bratislava, the Danube becomes the border between Slovakia and Hungary. By the time it reaches the city of Komaron, the river has slowed down a great deal. Even so, long barge trains heading upstream have to be split up as the current becomes too strong even for powerful pusher tugs. South of Komaron, the river is forced through a gap in the highlands of the Hungarian Central Massif and made to bend sharply to the south, through Budapest, Hungary's capital, and on for 150 km across the Great Hungarian Plain, or *Alföld* (often also called the *puszta*, meaning 'empty land').

This was once a huge inland sea which drained away down the route the Danube now follows, leaving behind a thick layer of alluvium which is ideal for farming. Much of the plain used to be marsh as it was regularly flooded by the Danube and its largest tributary, the Tisza, further to the east. Few people lived there, which is why it was referred to as the 'empty land'. In the last century, embankments and ditches were built to prevent the rivers overflowing and to drain the land. As the plain dried out, people moved there and began growing crops and breeding cattle and sheep.

This fertile flat land continues over the border into Croatia and Serbia, where numerous waterways, lined with thick forests, lead off the meandering main channel as the Danube heads across to Belgrade, the Serbian capital. Before reaching Belgrade, the Danube is joined by the Tisza and at Belgrade by the River Sava, another major tributary.

A ferry crossing-point in central Hungary. Ditches drain the marshes on either side of the river so that land can be farmed.

The lower Danube

Soon after Belgrade, the river becomes the border between Serbia, to the south, and Romania to the north, before entering one of the most impressive parts of its route — a succession of steep-sided gorges, eight in all, between the Carpathian and Yugoslavian Mountains. The gorges are usually referred to as the Iron Gates, though, in fact, this is the name of only the final and most dangerous gorge. This section of the river used to be the most hazardous, but thanks to a huge dam opened in 1971, it is now safe for boats of all sizes.

Leaving the Iron Gates behind, the Danube becomes the border between Romania and Bulgaria, before swinging north into Romania and then east to the Black Sea, skirting Ukraine to the north. There are no more highlands, just

The entrance to the Iron Gates gorges, with Romania on the left and Serbia on the right bank of the Danube. Dams have raised the water level, widening the river.

endless flat plains until the river arrives at its delta, a huge area of swamps, lagoons, sand dunes and floating islands of reeds among a maze of waterways, both natural and man-made.

Here, the Danube flows out into the Black Sea along three channels. Two of them, the Chilia and Sfintu Gheorghe channels, are old parts of the river. The third channel, leading to the port of Sulina, was straightened and deepened in the nineteenth century. It carries about 15 per cent of the Danube's water and so silts up more slowly than the other channels. For this reason it is the one most used by ships on their way into and out of the river. At present the channel is only 7 m deep, but there are plans to dredge out another 3 m so that large ships can travel upriver.

Below *These two huge, sea-going tugs can help any vessel in trouble on the Sulina channel in the delta.*

Above *The final stage of the Danube's journey: the main channel of the river at Tulcea, looking across the delta towards Sulina on the Black Sea.*

A Lipovani fisherman in one of the many channels of the delta.

Wildlife along the Danube

Over 70 types of fish live in the river, including a variety of salmon found nowhere else and giant catfish measuring up to 4 m long. In the forests along the banks roam deer, wild boar, wolves and foxes. Above them soar birds of prey, constantly on the look-out for small mammals hiding among the crops and the field hedgerows. Downriver from Hungary, many of the telegraph poles in riverside villages are topped with storks' nests.

The delta is world-famous for the different species of animals and plants that live there, many of which are not seen in other parts of Europe. Some 280 kinds of birds live either in the delta or stop over during their seasonal migrations. So important is the delta to naturalists that much of it is now a nature reserve where hunting is forbidden.

3. TAMING THE DANUBE

A wild river

Compared to its neighbour, the River Rhine, the Danube is little used. The Danube carries far fewer barges than the Rhine, which is one of the busiest waterways in the world. Why has the Danube not developed like the Rhine to become a major waterway for transporting cargoes?

One important reason is the character of the Danube itself. Until recent times, it was a very powerful and destructive river, because of the amount and the speed of the water flowing down it. If you stand by the side of the Rhine, just over 2,000 cubic metres of water will pass you every second. However, three times that amount would rush by if you stood on the banks of the Danube. Of course, this figure varies with the seasons. In the spring, when the melting snow of the Alps drains into the Danube through its many tributaries, the water level is very high. In the summer there is the opposite problem: too little water, so that boats run aground along some stretches of the river. The river is at its most dangerous when it is full of water, for then the current is very powerful.

Barges of all sizes can use the Danube in safety now, thanks to the series of dams which have reduced the destructive power of the river.

Now the waters are calm, but years ago, dangerous, swirling currents would have carried the river through this narrow, steep-sided gorge near Kelheim in southern Germany.

On its route to the Black Sea, the Danube passes through several narrow gorges, which constrict the water, creating terrific, swirling currents. Many of the gorges also contain large underwater rocks. Not only are these a hazard when the water is low, but during the high-water months, dangerous whirlpools are stirred up when the fast-flowing water collides with them. The currents, rocks and whirlpools used often to wreck boats or drag them and their crew to a watery grave.

In the winter, when there is little water and the river is flowing slowly, the Danube may freeze over, with a layer of ice thick enough to walk on. This only happens during very cold winters, which are less common now than in the past. Then, the Danube could be frozen for up to a month at a time and boats had to wait for the ice to thaw.

The Danube at Vienna. Earlier this century the river used to break its banks and flood the city. Now the river has been straightened to stop this happening.

All rivers carry sediment, but because the Danube has so many tributaries, it carries more than most. Some of it is dropped along the way and has to be cleared regularly to prevent the river becoming too shallow. The rest is taken down to the delta. Here, again, some is left in the channels leading to the mouths, clogging them up, so they have to be dredged frequently to keep them deep enough for ships. The sediment that remains is deposited at the mouths, increasing the delta's size.

All these problems have meant that travel along the Danube has been difficult and dangerous. This has affected the river's development as a major waterway. However, much has been done to remove many of the obstructions and hazards. Today's Danube is very different to the river of two hundred or even one hundred years ago. Like a wild animal, it has been tamed so that it can be put to good use.

Dangerous gorges

Two particular stretches of the Danube were once very hazardous for boats and barges. These were the Strudengau Gorge, south of Linz in Austria, and the Iron Gates Gorge on the borders of Romania and the former Yugoslavia. Both of them had to be made safer if more vessels were to use the river.

The small town of Grein stands at the entrance to the Strudengau Gorge. From earliest days, people travelling down the river would stop here to pray for a safe journey through the gorge and to take on board a pilot who could guide them through its tricky waters. Sometimes the pilot would consider conditions too perilous to proceed any further, so the boat would be unloaded and its cargo and passengers would continue overland to Vienna, where they would join another vessel. The gorge was full of huge underwater rocks, terrifying whirlpools

Opposite *The village of Grein, at the entrance to the Strudengau Gorge in Austria. People would stop here to pray for a safe journey through the treacherous gorge.*

and rapids where the current was very powerful: approaching any one of them from the wrong direction could result in disaster, and many a boat and its crew were lost.

In the 1700s, work began on clearing the gorge of all these obstacles. Tonnes of dynamite were used to blast away the sides to straighten it and to destroy the hidden rocks. The work continued well into the 1800s, but it was not until 1959, when the Ybbs-Persenbeug dam was completed, at the southern end of the gorge, that it became really safe. This dam slowed the current and raised the level of water so that the rocks were out of harm's way.

Even if a boat survived travelling through the Strudengau Gorge, the most difficult stretch of the river lay ahead — the Iron Gates Gorge. Here there were 125 km of even stronger currents and whirlpools, and huge underwater rocks. For hundreds of years, just mentioning the gorge's name was enough to send a shiver of terror down the spine of even the bravest of the Danube's sailors. In places, the current was so powerful that vessels heading downstream often went out of control; while those struggling upstream had to lighten their loads or be helped by a tug, whose engine could winch the boat along a cable laid on the river bed.

The Iron Gates Gorge, once one of the most difficult stretches of the Danube for sailors, now has few worries for them.

Much of this castle on the Serbian bank of the river has vanished beneath the lake created by the building of the Iron Gates dam.

Since the 1800s, much time and money had been spent on improving conditions in the gorge, but it remained a major hazard which would hinder any plans to increase the number of barges using the river. The only solution was yet another enormous dam to calm the river and make it deeper. Built jointly by Romania and Yugoslavia between 1960 and 1971, the Iron Gates Dam has solved all the navigation problems and provided both countries with huge amounts of hydro-electricity — but at a price. A long, thin lake now stretches for 100 km behind the dam, and beneath its waters lie whole islands, towns and villages. Over 23,000 people had to move to new homes higher up the valley sides, their old ones lost for ever. Even so, the formation of the lake has meant that travel along this part of the river is safer and quicker than ever before, two factors which have encouraged more businesses to use the Danube to transport their cargoes.

Locks have been built at each end of the dam at Aschach in Austria.

Damming the Danube

The dams at Ybbs-Persenbeug and the Iron Gates are just two in a chain of dams on the Danube which starts in Germany and ends in northern Hungary. There are five dams on the German section of the river, nine in Austria, two shared by Romania and Serbia, and a recently completed dam at Gabchikovo, in Slovakia, which is part of a plan to divert the main course of the Danube between Bratislava and Budapest. The dam is at the southern end of a 32-km, 20-m wide canal, which was opened in October 1992. Work on a dam at Cunovo, at the canal's northern end, has been halted following protests.

Dr Reinhold Christian

'I am a hydrologist and I advise the Austrian government about setting up a national park to protect endangered plants and animals living beside the Danube between Vienna and the Slovakian border. Pollution is not the problem because the river is quite clean here. Our main concern is to stop the river sinking. The Danube's fast rate of flow means that it digs into its bed at the rate of 2 cm a year. As a result the river banks are drying up and the plants and wildlife are suffering. We are trying to find the best way to halt this process.'

Dams and the environment

There have been arguments about the dams and canal in Slovakia since the beginning. Although the project would provide a lot of much-needed electricity and make travel easier on this section of the river, conservationists said that the large lake created by the Cunovo dam would drown an area in which many rare animals and plants lived. Slovakian farmers replied that because their soil was getting drier year by year, they needed to irrigate their fields and that the dams would help do this. Meanwhile, on the Hungarian side of the river, the farmers were worried that diverting the Danube through the new canal would dry up their fields so that no crops could be grown. Scientists, too, were concerned that the dams were being built in an area where earthquakes are common. These could destroy the dams and cause disaster.

The Slovakian dams have been so unpopular that plans to build one in Hungary have been abandoned.

Locks raise or lower the level of water so that vessels can pass through. This lock is on the Ybbs-Persenbeug dam, north of Vienna.

4. RIVER TRANSPORT

This exact copy of an early type of river boat called the Ulm Box is on the banks of the Danube at Ulm.

River travel in the past

Before the age of steam and the building of the dams, travel on the the Danube was mainly in one direction — downstream with the current. Going upstream, against the current, was an effort. Even the huge galleys of the Roman navy, with their two decks of rowers, and, later, the sail-powered warships of the Austrian and Hungarian navies, found it difficult, sometimes impossible, to travel against the current.

The earliest river craft were rafts, made of tree trunks lashed together, which drifted with the current, an oarsman at each end to steer them away from danger. At their destination, they would be broken up and the wood sold. Few of these rafts made the return journey because they required the hire of teams of horses and their handlers to pull them back upriver. Only a valuable cargo, like salt, would make such an expensive journey worthwhile. In the 1700s, a traveller on the Danube reported that the price of salt went up four times just to pay for the cost of the journey back.

The design of the rafts changed very little over the centuries. Even though they began to look more like boats, they were still very crude and simple — the most common type in the 1600s was called an Ulm Box. Built in the city after which they were named, 'box' was a good description for these flat-bottomed barges, with their draughty, hut-like cabins in the middle and a steering oar at either end. Crammed with people, cargo and animals, they floated downstream, using anchors to navigate through the dangerous sections. It was not a pleasant way to travel.

Conditions improved greatly in the 1800s with the arrival of larger, more comfortable, steam-driven ships. In 1830 a regular passenger service started between Vienna and Budapest. Four years later, steamships were travelling down to the Black Sea, as well as up the larger of the Danube's tributaries.

Vessels now had the power to travel against the strong current, so journeys could be made in both directions and tugs helped them through the difficult sections. Some ships were powered by paddle-wheels because they could work in water too shallow for propellers. Paddle-wheels, too, could get a better 'grip' in water disturbed by swirling currents.

This paddle-wheel tug Ruthoff *sank in 1944 after hitting a mine. It was rebuilt and worked on the middle Danube until the 1970s.*

River traffic today

Today ships are powered by diesel engines and improvements in the design of propellers have made paddle-wheels unnecessary. The river, too, has changed: dams have weakened the current and raised the water above the rocks, so the Danube can be used by craft of all sizes and for many purposes, particularly trade.

For most of its length, the Danube is too shallow for cargo ships. Instead, barges are used because they have flat bottoms and so need less depth of water.

A powerful pusher tug, with two huge barges in front, struggles upriver against the current at Vienna.

Below *Barges on the river at Budapest; one is lashed to the other to save fuel.*

26

Because of the marshy land there are few roads at the delta and many people use ferries for transport in the region.

They carry a variety of cargoes. The largest barges are 200 m long and 13 m wide, and capable of carrying 2,000 tonnes of cargo. Some of the barges have their own engines. Others have no engine and several are tied together and pushed by a tug, the whole formation being called a 'barge train'. In the delta, the channels are deep enough to be used by small ships. These sail up the channels from the Black Sea to unload their cargoes into barges, which take them upriver.

In much of the delta there are no roads or railways because the ground is marshy. The only way of getting about is by water. People use rowing boats for short trips, and launches, ships and fast hydrofoils for longer journeys. Further upriver, where land travel is not a problem, people need not rely on the river, so most passenger boats operate only in the summer to carry holidaymakers. In the summer, too, large 'botels' (short for boat hotels) travel along the river, stopping at historic places on the way.

The smallest craft on the Danube are those used for fun or for sports, like the weekend cabin cruisers, speedboats pulling waterskiers, yachts, sailboards, and canoes.

5. THE DANUBE IN HISTORY

The first settlers

While the Iron Gates Dam was being built, archaeologists worked busily in the areas that would soon be flooded by its lake. At Lepenski Vir, in Serbia, they excavated an 8,000-year-old town. The planning and building of its streets and houses had obviously been very carefully thought out. This discovery caused great excitement because it was the oldest town ever found. Previously it had been assumed that the 7,000-year-old cities of the Middle East had been the first towns, and that the idea of people settling down in one place to work or to farm instead of wandering around hunting and gathering food, had come from that region.

If the date is correct, then the people of Lepenski Vir were the first humans to travel on any of the world's rivers, perhaps on a raft made of tree trunks or a log hollowed out in the shape of a canoe. Even more important, their lifestyle and ideas (which were very advanced for the time) spread the length of the Danube's valley, influencing other communities and laying the foundations for European civilization.

The next settlers, the Celts, used the river to transport salt, iron and animal hides. After them came the Greeks, around 700 BC, but they stayed only on the lower Danube. By the time the Romans took control of the Danube, in about AD 200, the river had been a busy line of communication for a very long time, and not only did goods and people pass along it, but ideas as well. The Romans, however, found another role for the Danube, a military one.

This sculpture of a Roman galley shows the type of craft once used to patrol the Danube.

Roman rule

To the Romans, the Danube was little more than a huge water-filled ditch running down the eastern side of their empire, protecting them from the troublesome barbarians on the opposite side. Forts were built and supplied with troops and provisions by boat. To protect the boats, fleets of galleys of the Roman navy began to patrol the river, and harbours and shipyards were opened where the galleys could anchor and be repaired. As well as improving the facilities along the river, the Romans also built good roads so that their legions could march quickly to trouble spots.

After the collapse of the Roman Empire, about AD 476, the roads fell into disrepair, encouraging more people to travel along the Danube. Dangerous though this was, it was safer for travellers than going by land, where, even if they survived the terrible roads, bands of highwaymen took their belongings — if not their lives.

Above *The Nemesis twins – a Roman sculpture discovered in Romania by archaeologists. The statues were probably decorations in a temple.*

Left *This Roman frieze was discovered by archaeologists in the lower Danube region, showing how far the Roman Empire stretched.*

29

Crusaders on the river

As business built up on the Danube, the powerful barons and bishops in charge of riverside towns realized that there was money to be made from passing merchants and travellers, so they began charging them a tax for using their stretch of the river.

During the Middle Ages, many of the people who paid this toll were on their way to the Crusades in the Holy Land (now Israel and Jordan) and the Danube was the quickest route. The most famous Crusader was King Richard I of England, who was imprisoned in Dürnstein Castle, south of Linz, by King Leopold V of Austria. According to legend, Richard was rescued by his faithful minstrel, Blondel, after recognizing the song Blondel was singing beneath his window.

The main aim of the Crusades had been to drive the Turks out of the Holy Land to weaken the Turkish Empire. When the Crusaders failed to do this, Turkish armies began marching on south-eastern Europe and by the end of the Middle Ages, Turkey controlled much of the middle and lower Danube. Once again, the Danube had become the frontier of an empire.

Above *This modern statue of Richard I and the minstrel Blondel is near the remains of Dürnstein Castle, Austria, where the king was imprisoned.*

While the Turks were in power, travellers and traders were discouraged from using the river. But matters improved in the late 1600s, after the Turks had been driven out by Austria's armies. For the next two hundred years and more, most of the Danube became part of the Austro-Hungarian Empire, ruled from Vienna by the Habsburg kings and queens.

Left *An old manuscript painting showing Crusaders making their way to the Holy Land.*

The Royal Palace on the Buda side of the river in Budapest. It was built by the Austrian Habsburgs and then destroyed by the German army in 1944. It has now been rebuilt.

A river divided

The Austro-Hungarian Empire was broken up in 1918, at the end of the First World War, and many new countries were created, including Czechoslovakia, Romania and Yugoslavia.

In 1946, after the Second World War, an 'Iron Curtain' came down across Europe, separating the West from the countries in the East, which were controlled by what was once the USSR. The upper part of the Danube was in the West and the middle and lower parts of the river were in the East. The 'Cold War' between the East and the West (lasting from 1945–90) meant that there was little trade between the two and, as a result, the development of the Danube for shipping was held up.

With the break-up of the USSR into independent states, in the early 1990s, the 'Iron Curtain' has finally fallen, so there is no longer this barrier to progress. The countries in the former East have been slow to develop. Set free from the USSR, they are now trying to catch up with the West. As their industries are modernized, trade with the rest of Europe will increase: this will mean more business for the Danube's barges in the years to come.

Mauthausen concentration camp
Few people would have heard of the sleepy little village of Mauthausen, on the banks of the Danube in Austria, were it not for the concentration camp built there by Adolf Hitler. Many similar camps were set up all over Europe between 1933 and 1945, where Hitler imprisoned and put to death people from inside and outside Germany. More than 100,000 people died in Mauthausen concentration camp. The camp has been left as a memorial to them and as a warning to future generations not to let such terrible atrocities happen again.

6. CAPITAL CITIES

Along its route the Danube passes the capital cities of three countries: Vienna in Austria, Budapest in Hungary, and Belgrade in Serbia (formerly the capital of Yugoslavia).

Vienna

Vienna has always been an important city because of its location. Almost in the centre of Europe, it was once at the crossroads of two major trade routes. From the north came Viking traders with furs, iron, and precious Baltic amber, heading south to the markets on the Mediterranean. They were joined from the east by merchants with valuable spices and silk, travelling west along the Danube's valley.

The Romans called Vienna Vindobona and built a large fortress to protect their frontier from attack by Attila the Hun from the east. In the ninth century AD, Vienna marked the limits of another empire, this time the Frankish empire of Charlemagne. Eight hundred years later, the city nearly became part of the Turkish Empire in south-eastern Europe, but managed to fight off the Turkish army in 1683.

By then, Vienna was the capital of the Austro-Hungarian Empire and it soon became one of the most talked-about

The rooftops of central Vienna, home of the composer Johann Strauss, whose Blue Danube Waltz *has made the river famous all over the world.*

The impressive buildings of the Hungarian Parliament on the Pest side of the river, where most of the businesses are located in Budapest.

cities in Europe. In its famous coffee-houses, some of Europe's finest musicians would meet (they included Mozart, Haydn and Beethoven), and writers and scholars including Sigmund Freud (who investigated the workings of the human mind).

In 1945, at the end of the Second World War, Vienna once again became a frontier city, when Europe was split into the East and the West, separated by the 'Iron Curtain'. Nowadays Vienna is a stepping-off point into Hungary and the Czech and Slovak republics.

Belgrade is the least attractive of the three capital cities on the Danube, perhaps because it has been destroyed and rebuilt so many times.

Budapest

Like Vienna, Budapest was an important part of the *limes* (the Roman name for the line of forts along the Danube). The city is really two towns, each with a different character, separated by the river. Buda is built on the hilly west side, where the Romans originally settled, and Pest is on the flat land on the opposite bank. While Buda became the town from which the country was governed and the home of the royal family, Pest developed as a centre for business and trade. The two were linked only by boat until 1840, when the first bridge was built. Thirty years later, the two towns joined together and their names combined into one word.

Today, without doubt, Budapest is the most important city in Hungary. All the country's financial institutions and many of its large industries are based there. It has Hungary's only civil airport and all the main roads and railways either start in or pass through the city. Budapest also leads all the other Hungarian cities in fashion, theatre, music and literature.

Belgrade

The nation of Yugoslavia came into existence after the First World War, when six small states joined together. Serbia was the largest state and its capital, Belgrade, also became the capital of Yugoslavia. In 1991, war broke out between the states and most have become independent. At the present time, all that is left of Yugoslavia are the states of Serbia and Montenegro.

In the past, many armies have tried to capture Belgrade because of its strategic position, situated at the point where two large rivers, the Sava and Danube, meet. Whoever controls Belgrade can watch both rivers and control who uses them. Belgrade has been destroyed and rebuilt so many times that people have lost count. With good road, rail and river links to other parts of what was formerly Yugoslavia, and to neighbouring countries, many important industries developed in Belgrade, providing jobs for a quarter of the population. However, when civil war broke out in Yugoslavia in 1991, the social and economic effects for Belgrade were disastrous.

7. INDUSTRIES

Shipbuilding

Not surprisingly, one of the important industries on the Danube is connected with the river itself — building all the vessels that are used on it. Barges, ferries, tugs; and passenger, cargo, naval and cruise ships, are all built along the Danube. These are constructed in shipyards at Korneuburg, just north of Vienna in Austria, at Komaron and Budapest in Hungary, and at Giurgiu, Galati and Tulcea in Romania. The shipyards build the hulls of the vessels and other firms supply the engines, fittings and equipment for the interiors.

Iron and steel

The manufacture of iron and steel is another major industry. There are steel foundries at Linz in Austria, Dunaujavros in Hungary, and Galati in Romania. These have been built on the riverbank because transporting the raw materials is easier by river than by road or rail. Most of the iron ore, as well as the coal needed to heat the furnaces in which the ore is turned into metal, comes from other countries and arrives by ship at one of the ports in the Danube delta. Barges are the cheapest way of getting these materials to the foundries upriver.

At Krems harbour near Vienna, trains and trucks bring containers which are then loaded on to barges and transported along the river.

Barges are also used to transport the manufactured metal, which is produced in long strips or wide sheets, too bulky to transport by road or rail, but presenting few problems for barges.

Many factories have been built alongside the Danube. Some use the river water in the manufacturing process or empty factory waste into the river, or they may use the river to transport the raw materials they need or the goods they produce. Danube industries include chemical and fertilizer production, and oil and petrol refineries.

This chemical factory has recently been built near Kelheim in Germany. The factory uses water from the Danube.

Captain Otto Ziehengraser

'I am the captain of the *Mozart*, the pride of the First Danube Steamship Company, based in Vienna. My ship is 121 m long and 23 m wide, and is the largest river passenger ship in Europe, providing 212 people with all the comforts of a top-class hotel. The *Mozart* travels the length of the Danube, from Passau to the delta. All the dams have made my job easier, because the current is now slower and the water level is always constant. Even so, we have a pilot to guide us, who knows the river very well. I use the radio to warn ships to keep clear when we are approaching a bend or a tricky narrow section.'

Tourism

Finally, there is the tourist industry. People come on holiday from all over the world to visit the towns, cities and historic places beside the Danube. They stay in hotels, eat in restaurants, buy souvenirs, take coach trips and cruise in river boats. Tourism in the region earns a lot of money and provides many people with jobs.

Above *River cruises and souvenir shops are both important to the tourist industry along the Danube.*

The delta's reeds

There is a special industry in the delta which uses the reeds growing on the islands. Once, the reeds were cut down to make fences and roofs. Nowadays, they are used to produce paper, cardboard, alcohol and fertilizer. Anything left over is compressed into log shapes for burning in stoves. Altogether, 200,000 tonnes of reeds are harvested each year. The main problem is that harvesting the reeds has to be done by hand, as the ground is too soft for machines.

8. POWER AND POLLUTION

Water for power

Much of the power for the Danube's industries is provided by the river, because the dams across it have been built for two purposes. The first is to make the river deeper and easier for boats to travel on. The second is to supply hydro-electricity, using the power of the river's current to turn turbines for generating electricity, which can then be taken to factories.

The Iron Gates Dam is the best example of a dam which combines both these functions. Not only has it removed many hazards along the river, but its twelve huge turbines (six at either end) provide enormous amounts of electricity for Romania and the former Yugoslavia.

This electricity is badly needed as both Romania and the states which made up the former Yugoslavia have energy shortages which are holding up the development of their industries and cities.

Water for cooling

The Danube's water is also used for cooling the reactors in nuclear power plants. The biggest nuclear reactor on the Danube is at Cernavoda in Romania. When it is finished, it will supply nearly 25 per cent of the country's electricity. Another large reactor, at Kozloduj, provides Bulgaria with nearly 50 per cent of its energy needs.

The huge Iron Gates dam supplies Romania and the states of the former Yugoslavia with much-needed electricity for their homes and factories.

Huge steel-making plants, like this one at Tulcea in the Danube delta, discharge waste material into the river, adding to the pollution.

Pollution of the Danube

Factories and nuclear power plants are the greatest source of pollution of the Danube. Until recent times, the countries of Eastern Europe cared little about what was dumped in the river or about the dangerous gases belching out of factory chimneys. Eastern European governments are more concerned now and are trying to reduce air and river pollution. Although the people of the Danube countries are angry that industries continue to empty their poisonous wastes into the river, they are even more worried about the dangers caused by nuclear reactors.

Kozloduj, for example, was recently described by a scientist as 'one of the most dangerous places in Europe'. The nuclear reactor had been so badly built and poorly maintained that highly radioactive chemicals, such as cobalt and caesium, were leaking into the canals which carried its cooling water to and from the Danube. To make matters worse, local farmers used water from the canals on their crops. Thus the reactor is harming both the environment and people's health.

The Austrians have been more fortunate. So many people objected to the new nuclear reactor at Zwentendorf, on the river just north of Vienna, that the Austrian government held a referendum to decide what to do with it. A majority voted against it, so the reactor will never be used, even though it has been built.

Generating electricity
Countries cannot survive without electricity because it is needed to power almost everything, from lighting in houses to machines in factories. But what is the best way of obtaining it?
● Nuclear power stations use harmful radioactive chemicals which are difficult to destroy, and accidents can result in disasters.
● Power stations using coal are less dangerous, but produce gases which damage the atmosphere and affect the climate.
● Dams, too, disrupt the environment by flooding huge areas and drowning towns and the habitats of rare species of animals and plants.

Until alternative forms of energy, like wind or solar power, can supply us with enough electricity, traditional ways of generating it will have to be used, even though each has its problems.

9. FARMING AND FISHING

Farming on the upper Danube

As it flows through the gently rolling hills of southern Germany, most of the farmland on the banks of the Danube is used for growing crops. These are mainly wheat and rye. The farmers also plant vegetables, make cheese, and breed pigs for the sausages and ham which the Germans enjoy so much. The Germans are also great beer drinkers and most of the hops, which give beer its bitter taste, are cultivated in this part of the country.

For much of its route through Austria, the river snakes between high hills, covered with forests. Where the lower slopes of the hillsides have been cleared of trees, the farmers grow fruit (including apples, pears, plums and peaches) and grapes for making wine. Some of the best wines in Austria are produced in the beautiful Wachau Valley, between Linz and Vienna. The Danube has a continental climate, which means that summers are hot and winters cold. So the farmers have to watch out for frosts in spring which may harm the young buds on the vines.

Grapes growing on the hillsides of the Wachau Valley in Austria. Most of them will be used to make the wine for which this region is famous.

Erich Salomon

'My family has been making wine at the Undhof vineyard in Krems, in the Wachau Valley, for seven generations. The soil and climate here are good for growing grapes, so it produces some of the best wines in Austria. We have a medium-sized vineyard, about 22 ha in all, from which we produce 150,000 bottles a year of good-quality white wine. Most of the wine is sold to hotels and restaurants in Austria.'

The Great Plain of Hungary

Most of the Danube's middle course is across the flatlands of central and southern Hungary, called the Great Plain. This inland sea, which existed millions of years ago, eventually drained away, leaving behind a fine sandy soil which had been carried down by rivers from the surrounding mountains. Parts of the Great Plain are also covered in loess — tiny particles of mud and clay which have been blown by the wind from the Russian steppes, far to the east. The loess and the soil of the old sea-bed are excellent for farming, so many different crops are grown, including grains (such as corn, wheat, barley and rye), sugar beet, fruit and the paprikas for which Hungary is famous. In the summer, crops may be damaged by the strong, hot winds which blow across the Great Plain.

This small farm is one of hundreds dotted all over Hungary's Great Plain.

Ferenc Szücs

'I used to be one of the famous cowboys on the *puszta*, the Great Plain of Hungary. I would spend the summer months on horseback, herding a large flock of sheep. Now I have retired to my smallholding, where I keep sheep and a few pigs. I sell the sheep and their lambs, but keep the pigs for their meat. I also have a small vineyard nearby, which provides me with enough wine for a year. The soil on the *puszta* is very fertile and maize, sunflowers and all sorts of fruit and vegetables are grown, many for sale in Budapest.'

Farming along the lower Danube

The rich soils of the Hungarian plain extend across the border into Croatia and Serbia, where there are vineyards and orchards on the low hills alongside the river. Vegetables and grains also grow.

After passing through the steep-sided Iron Gates Gorge, the Danube's valley flattens out again for the final part of its journey to the Black Sea. The soil consists of layers of fertile alluvium left by the river after it has flooded over its banks. There is little industry in Romania and Bulgaria, so farming is still very important. Grains, sunflowers, sugar beet, tobacco, cotton and hemp are the main crops. The summers are very hot here and there is little rain, rarely more than 500 mm a year. In some years there are droughts, with no rain for months on end. When this happens the harvest is ruined, unless water can be taken from the river.

The Danube delta has been built up over the centuries by the silt dumped by the river as it enters the Black Sea. Vegetables, like tomatoes, paprikas and onions, and fruit, especially melons, are grown on the islands which are not marsh.

A fruit and vegetable stall in the centre of Budapest. Everything will have been grown on the Great Plain.

Fishing in the delta

Besides farming, many people in the delta earn a living from catching fish such as catfish, bream, carp, perch and sturgeon. The eggs of the sturgeon are called caviare and they are sold abroad for a very high price. Large frogs, too, are caught and their legs sent to France and Italy, where people enjoy eating them.

A fisherman in the Danube delta examines one of his nets to see if he has caught anything. The channels and lakes of the delta teem with many different types of fish.

10. LOOKING AHEAD

Linking the North and Black Seas

For centuries, people have thought about ways of connecting Europe's rivers to make it possible to travel by water from the North Sea to the Black Sea. Until 1992, this journey could only be done by way of the Atlantic Ocean and the Mediterranean Sea. But in September of that year a canal was opened which joined the River Main, a tributary of the River Rhine, to the Danube. This allowed barges to travel from Rotterdam, on the North Sea coast, to Sulina, on the Black Sea. The completion of the Danube-Black Sea Canal in 1984 also means that barges or small ships can avoid the delta and go directly to the Black Sea port of Constanta.

The idea of linking the Main and Danube rivers was not new: Emperor Charlemagne had tried to do it in AD 793. But the sides of his 9-metre-wide, 3-metre-deep ditch kept collapsing and the project was halted after two months' back-breaking work by an army of men.

Just over a thousand years later, King Ludwig I of Bavaria decided to try again. Thousands of men began work in 1837, after engineers had spent four years planning the route. Ten years later, a canal between Bamberg, on the River Main, and Kelheim, on the Danube, was finished. It was 172 km long, 10.5 m wide and 1.5 m deep, complete with 101 locks to raise barges 457 m over the hills, Ludwig was justifiably proud of his canal.

To get over the highest point on the Main-Danube Canal, barges have to be lifted up in 45 locks: an amazing engineering feat.

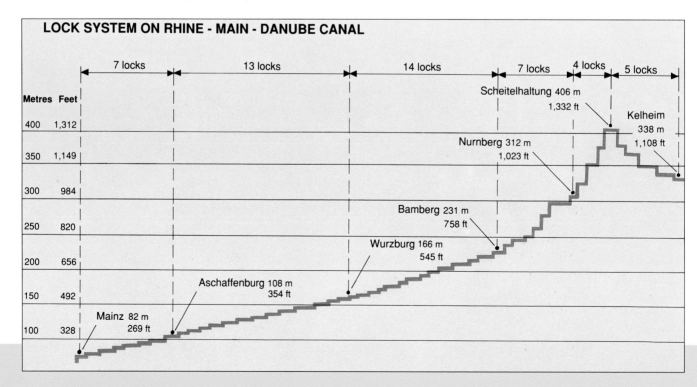

LOCK SYSTEM ON RHINE - MAIN - DANUBE CANAL

A barge on the River Main near Frankfurt. Thanks to the new Main-Danube Canal, boats can now travel all the way to the Black Sea, along the Rhine-Danube Waterway.

Although it was an amazing engineering achievement, Ludwig's Canal was not a business success. The age of steam had arrived and it became quicker to send goods by rail, especially as the canal frequently dried up for months on end. In 1921 the German government decided to build a bigger and better canal which would earn money from the barges paying to use it, as well as from selling the electricity generated by the turbines in the dams along it. The canal opened seventy-one years later.

Engineering problems, lack of money and opposition from local people and environmental groups had all delayed the project.

Right from the start, many conservationists have argued against the building of the new canal, saying that it is not needed and that it will harm one of the last unspoilt areas of Germany. The canal's builders have replied that, with its opening, more businesses will start sending their goods by water all over Europe. Everyone will benefit from this because it is the form of transport which pollutes the atmosphere the least.

The builders have listened to the conservationists' arguments and have designed the canal so that it will disrupt the countryside as little as possible. They have also built backwaters and lakes so that the wildlife can remain undisturbed.

The new canal should be good for the future of the Danube. The industries in the centre of Europe and in the CIS are connected, which will boost the trade of materials best carried on water. Looking further ahead, there are even plans to link the Danube to the Baltic Sea with a waterway from Bratislava to the River Elbe. After being little used for centuries, there is a busy time ahead for the River Danube.

GLOSSARY

Alluvium Fertile soil that has been formed from all the material deposited by a river.

Archaeologists People who study objects and remains from ancient times.

Barbarians Primitive brutal people.

Barge A flat-bottomed boat used on rivers and canals.

Canal A man-made waterway.

CIS Commonwealth of Independent States, which includes Russia and other former republics of the USSR.

Cold War The state of hostility and tension that existed between America and her allies, and the USSR and its satellite countries, lasting from the end of the Second World War in 1945 until 1990.

Confluence The point where two rivers meet.

Conservationists People who try to protect and care for the environment.

Crusades Expeditions during the Middle Ages, when Christian soldiers (Crusaders) tried to recapture the Holy Land from the Muslims.

Delta A flat, fan-shaped area where a river splits into many channels at the end of its course.

Dredge To dig out mud and silt from a river bed.

Embankment An artificial bank of earth or stone designed to prevent a river from flooding.

Excavate To dig up buried objects from the earth to obtain information about the past.

Galley A long, low ship powered by oars and a sail.

Geological To do with the scientific study of the history and structure of the Earth.

Gorge A narrow, steep-sided valley.

Hazardous Risky or dangerous.

Hitler, Adolf The dictator who ruled Germany from 1933–45. He ordered the building of concentration camps where Jews, and other people whom he disliked, were exterminated, and he invaded neighbouring countries, bringing about the Second World War (1939–45).

Hull The main body of a boat or ship.

Hydro-electricity Electricity generated by the power of falling water.

Hydrofoils Light, fast vessels which travel over the surface of the water on a type of stilts.

Hydrologist Someone who studies the Earth's water.

Irrigate To supply land with water.

Lock A section of a canal or river that may be closed off to control the water level and the raising and lowering of boats that pass through.

Marsh Swampy, wet land.

Meandering Taking a winding course.

Migrations Regular movements of birds and animals from one area to another.

Referendum A vote taken by all the people in a country to decide a course of action.

Sediment Material such as clay, sand or stones, that is carried by a river and then deposited.

Silt Very fine particles of soil and rock carried by a river.

Species Different types of animals or plants.

Steppes Extensive grasslands, especially in south-eastern Europe and western Asia.

Strategic To be in a well-placed position.

Toll A fee charged to vehicles or ships before they can use certain stretches of road, bridge or waterway.

Tributaries Streams and rivers that feed a larger river.

Waterway A route on a river or canal that can be used by barges or small ships.

Winch To haul along a machine-operated cable.

FURTHER READING

The Danube by R. Heikell (Imray, 1991)
The Danube by C. A. R. Hills (Wayland, 1979)
Great Rivers of the World ed. by Alexander Frater (Hodder and Stoughton, 1984)

Further information about the history and cultures along the Danube can be obtained from the nearest tourist offices of the following countries: Austria, Bulgaria, Germany, Hungary and Romania.

Acknowledgements
The author would like to thank the following for their help and advice: Ursula Deutsch, General Secretary of the Danube Tourist Commission, Vienna; Dr Joszef Czegledi and Mrs Pollak of the Hungarian Tourist Office; Traian Arhip and Mrs Pencea of the Romanian Tourist Office; Gerwald Dvorak of the DDSG-Donaureisen (the First Danube Steamship Company); and Rhein-Main-Donau AG.

Picture acknowledgements
All photographs including the cover are by David Cumming except the following: Tony Stone Worldwide 19 (Tony Craddock); Zefa 17 (K. Jung), 20, 34; Wayland Picture Library 28, 30 (lower). The map on page 5 is by Peter Bull. Artwork on pages 6, 9 and 45 is by John Yates.

INDEX

Numbers in **bold** refer to illustrations